नंबरों की कहानी

THE NUMBER STORY

SMALL BOOK ONE

ENGLISH - HINDI

Numbers Teach Children
Their Number Names

written and illustrated by

MISS ANNA

Early Reader Edition of *The Number Story 1*
Bronze Medal Winner, 2016 Wishing Shelf Book Award

Copyright © 2018 by Jieeun Woo
Illustrations © Jieeun Woo

Cover by | Lumpy Publishing
Layout by | Lumpy Publishing
Translated by Mitesh Soni & Linguainfo Services Pvt. Ltd.
Coloring by Jieeun Woo and Maria Mirabella

All rights reserved. No part of this book may be reproduced or transmitted in any form or by any means whatsoever, including photocopying, recording or by any information storage and retrieval system, without written permission from the publisher and/or author: missanna@missannabooks.com.

Library of Congress Control Number: 2018902040

Names: Miss Anna, author.
Title: Number story : numbers teach children their number names / Miss Anna.
Description: Portland, OR: Lumpy Publishing, 2018.
Identifiers: ISBN 978-1-945977-21-3 | LCCN 2018902040
Summary: The pictures and rhymes present stories which introduce numbers 0-10.
Subjects: LCSH Numeration—English--Hindi--Pictorial works--Juvenile literature. | BISAC JUVENILE NONFICTION /
Languages: English--Hindi
Classification: LCC QA141.3 .M57 2018 | DDC 513—dc23

Publisher: Lumpy Publishing
Website: www.missannabooks.com
Email: missanna@missannabooks.com

Paperback: ISBN 978-1-945977-21-3
Printed in the U.S.A.   1 3 5 7 9 10 8 6 4 2

क्या आप हमारे नंबरों
के नाम सीखना चाहेंगे?

It is very easy and a lot of fun!

यह काफी आसान है और बहुत मजेदार भी!

Say-along our little jingle

छोटी सी कहानी हमारे साथ गाएं!

starting from Number One!

नंबर एक से शुरू करते है!

1

ONE looks like my one finger.

१ ☆ एक

एक उंगली जैसी लगती है।

ONE!
एक!

2

TWO   trails a tail.

२ दो

दो एक पूंछ का पीछा।

एक पूंछ!

3

THREE has bumps.

३ ☆ तीन

तीन में बंप है।

BUMPY!

ऊबड़ खाबड़!

4

FOUR   carries a sail.

४ ☆ चार

चार जहाज ले जाता है।

A SAIL!
एक जल यात्रा!

5

FIVE   is a racing track.

५ पाँच

पाँच एक रेसिंग ट्रैक है।

VROOM!
बूम!

6

SIX curves like a snail.

६ ☆ छह

छह घोंघे की तरह गोल है।

A SNAIL!

एक घोंघा !

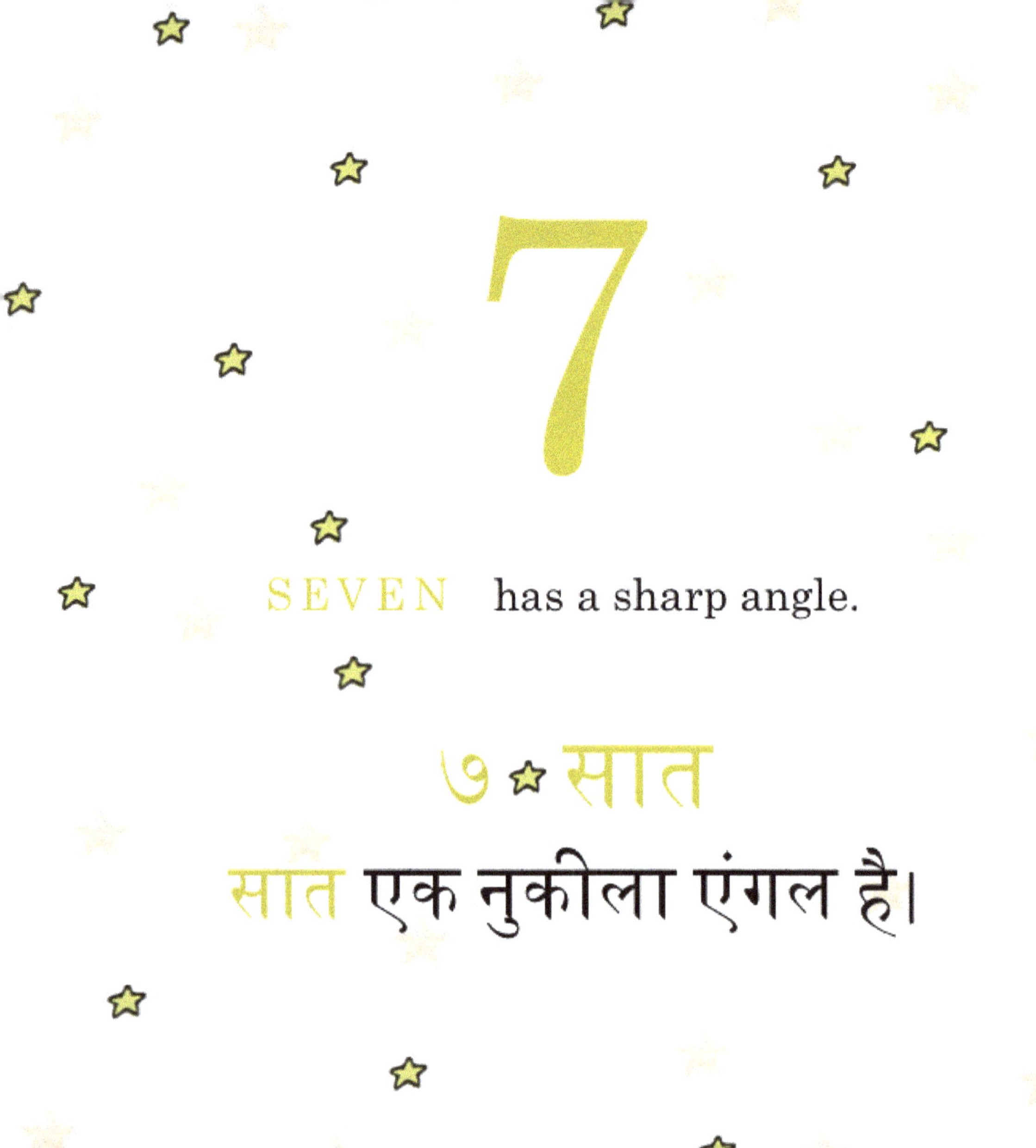
7

SEVEN   has a sharp angle.

७ ✦ सात
सात एक नुकीला एंगल है।

BE CAREFUL! IT'S SHARP!
सावधान! यह नुकीला है!

8
EIGHT   is rollercoaster rails.
८ ✦ आठ
आठ एक रोलरकोस्टर रेल है।

वाह!
YIPPEE!

9

 is a bubble on a stick.

९ ☆ नौ

नौ मानो छड़ी पर एक बुलबुला है।

A BUBBLE! एक बुलबुला!

10

TEN   is an eye of a whale.

१० ☆ दस

दस व्हेल की एक आँख है।

पलक पलक!
WINK!

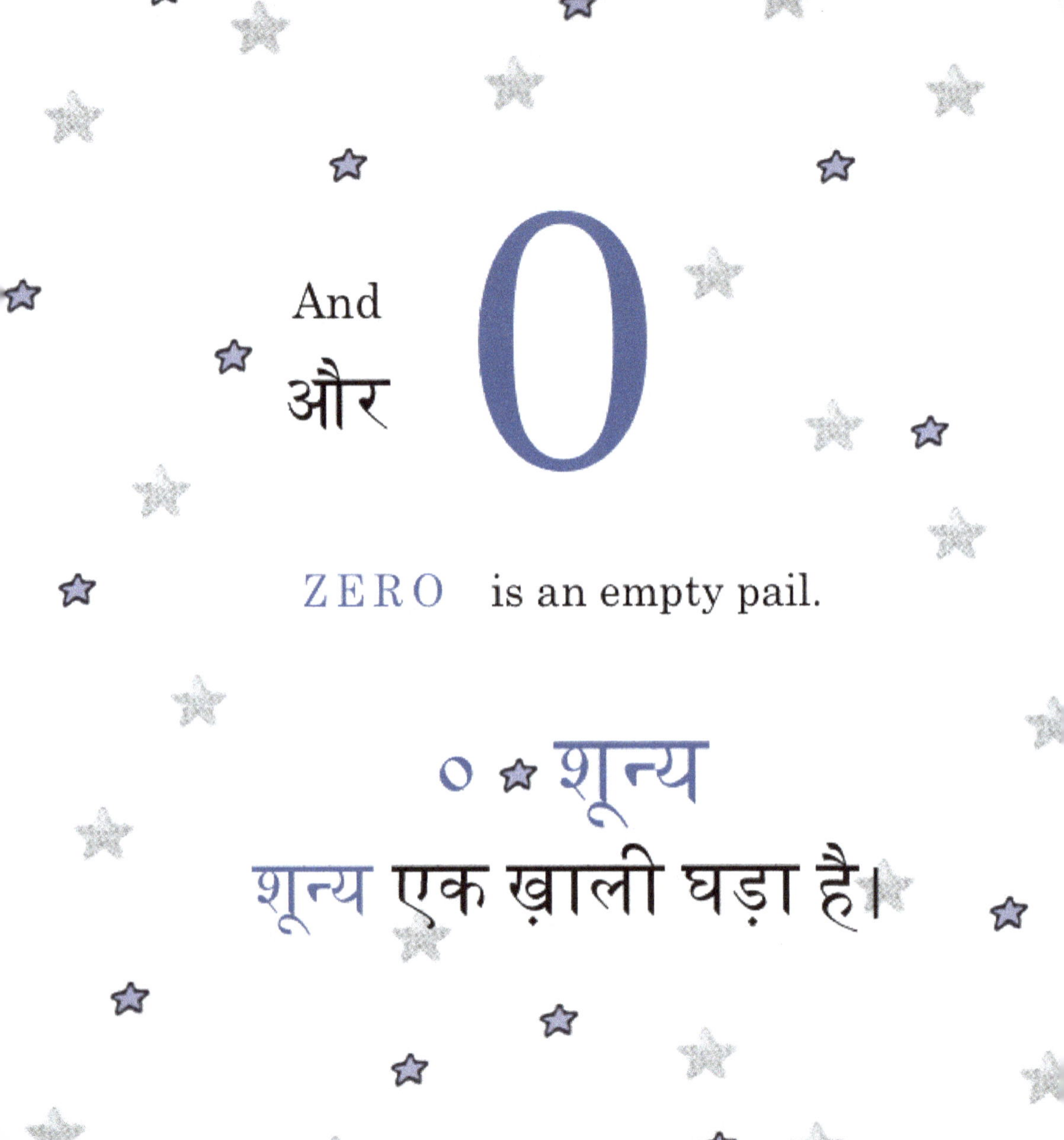
And
और

0

ZERO   is an empty pail.

० ☆ शून्य

शून्य एक ख़ाली घड़ा है।

IT'S EMPTY!
यह है खाली!

Thank you for playing with us today.

We had a lot of fun too!

आज हमारे साथ खेलने के लिए शुक्रिया।
हमें भी बहुत मज़ा आया!

We are your Number friends,
Zero to Ten,
Who will be here for you~

हम आपके नंबर मित्र है
शून्य से दस।
हम हमेशा ही रहेंगे आपके साथ!

Bye-bye now!
See you again soon!

अभी के लिए विदा!
जल्द मिलेंगे दोबारा!

The Numbers are *SINGING* too!

To sing-a-long, look for Miss Anna Number Story
at your favorite music store like iTUNES.

MP3

Numbers 0-10
IDENTIFYING
& COUNTING

Numbers 11-20
& Ordinals

first, second, third...

Numbers 0-100
& Place Values

ones, tens, hundreds...

About Clocks
& Telling Time

hours, minutes, seconds

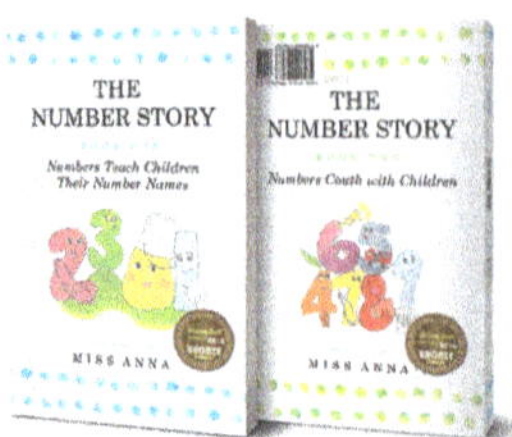

Number Story 1 & 2

isbn: 978-0-996216-48-7

Number Story 3 & 4

isbn: 978-1-945977-01-5

Number Story 5 & 6

isbn: 978-1-945977-06-0

Number Story 7 & 8

isbn: 978-1-949320-40-4

For more Miss Anna books to love,
visit us at

w w w . m i s s a n n a b o o k s . c o m

Numbers are working hard all over the world!
Come Travel the World with Us!

www.ingramcontent.com/pod-product-compliance
Lightning Source LLC
Chambersburg PA
CBHW040901070726
47599CB00035B/2259